ARIANA GRANDE

YOUR ESSENTIAL, UNOFFICIAL GUIDE TO THE SUPERSTAR

DEAN

First published in Great Britain 2019 by Dean,
part of Egmont Books

An imprint of HarperCollins*Publishers*
1 London Bridge Street, London SE1 9GF
www.egmontbooks.co.uk

HarperCollins*Publishers*
1st Floor, Watermarque Building, Ringsend Road
Dublin 4, Ireland

Written by Malcolm Mackenzie
Designed by Ian Pollard

100% Unofficial Ariana Grande © Egmont Books 2019

ISBN 978 1 4052 9595 6
Printed in Italy
6

Egmont takes its responsibility to the planet and its inhabitants very
seriously. We aim to use papers from well-managed forests run by
responsible suppliers.

ARIANA GRANDE

YOUR ESSENTIAL, UNOFFICIAL GUIDE TO THE SUPERSTAR

Malcolm Mackenzie

CONTENTS

THIS IS ME

ARIANA GRANDE

If you stan the Dangerous Woman, here's the basics you really should know

NAME: Ariana Grande Butera

BIRTHDAY: 26 June 1993

STAR SIGN: Cancer – the most caring and sensitive zodiac sign.

BORN: Boca Raton, Florida, USA.

HEIGHT: 5ft nothing.

FAVOURITE COLOUR HISTORY: It was lavender, then yellow, now it's ice blue/grey – specific, right?

TV: Ari loves *Grey's Anatomy*, *Planet Earth*, *RuPaul's Drag Race*, *American Horror Story*, and *America's Next Top Model*.

BOOK: *God Wears Lipstick* - she reads it over and over again. She also adores a certain Harry Potter.

MOVIE: *Bruce Almighty*. She also has a thing for horror films.

DRINK: Starbucks iced soy latte, Pink Veuve Cliquot champagne

FOOD: Because Ariana is a vegan, she eats no meat or dairy preferring to snack on beans, veg, fruits, nuts, rice, tofu and medjool dates. Yummers.

GAMES: Monopoly, ice hockey, Pokémon GO.

BAD HABITS: She cracks her knuckles all the time.

CRITTERS: "I love animals more than I love most people, not kidding."

WEATHER: Foggy rainy days.

INFLUENCES: India Irie, Whitney Huston, Beyoncé, Diana Ross, Donna Summer and Imogen Heap.

ROLE MODEL: Madonna, "She is my idol as far as attitude. I just love how she stands up for what she believes in."

CHARITY: Ariana formed *Kids Who Care* – a youth singing group when she was just 10 years old.

CRUSH: Ariana says she wrote a song for Harry Potter actor Tom Felton who played Draco Malfoy when she was 9 years old – hisssssssssss.

10 ARIANA SECRETS

SHHHHH

Don't say we told you, but did you know ...?

1
Everyone says her surname wrong. According to Ariana, her Grandpa pronounced their name 'Grandee' and that's how she pronounced it growing up.

2
You can watch ye olde videos from Ariana's original YouTube channel at Osnapitzari (Oh snap! It's Ari – geddit?)

3
Ariana loves Halloween so much that she's been known to decorate her house and leave it like that – FOR MONTHS afterwards.

4
The first song Ari remembers singing was *Somewhere Over The Rainbow* and the first song she ever wrote was about rain – coincidence?

5
Sony didn't go ahead and sign Ariana – seriously. Can you imagine?!

6
Her eyesight is so terrible, she's been dubbed 'the queen of squinting.'

7
There's a reason Ariana lives in a house full of dogs: she's allergic to cats.

8
Ariana is a gifted mimic and her impersonations of Britney, Shakira, Rihanna, Christina and Whitney are next level unbelievable.

9
Ariana would rather we all forget about her first single *Put Your Hearts Up*, describing it as "inauthentic and fake."

10
Justin Bieber's manager Scooter Braun saw Ariana's cover of the Justin Bieber song *Die In Your Arms* on YouTube in 2012, and had to sign her. Sensible man.

THE ROAD TO
NICKELODEON

It wasn't all plain sailing, but with hard work Ariana Grande started to make an impression

Annie Time

When Ariana was 8 years old she auditioned for her first singing gig, a role in a local production of *Annie*. She got the part and never looked back, appearing in community theatre productions of *Beauty and The Beast* and *The Wizard of Oz*.

TOTALLY BRASSED OFF

Ariana has revealed that she never had singing lessons but she did learn a musical instrument growing up: the French horn. She took lessons for years, which helped her learn to read music and understand song craft.

To offer some emotional support, Ariana's mum had a small part in Annie too. She played Daddy Warbucks' maid.

Ariana and 13 co-star and childhood friend Aaron Simon Gross in 2009.

13 Reasons Why

Ariana couldn't believe it when she beat thousands of wannabes to secure a part in the Broadway musical 13, and even though she didn't have many lines, she got to sing all the super high parts – of course! It was here that she learned to sing properly, challenge herself and expand her vocal range.

ARI SAYS

"I went right from middle school, like regular, everyday school, to Broadway. And that was a really crazy transition to make because it was so much hard work. I was like 'yay, no more school!' Then I was like oh my God, I have to kill myself every day dancing for more than 12 hours."

ARI SIGNED WITH REPUBLIC RECORDS IN 2011

Victorious, a teen comedy set in a performing arts high school, ran for four seasons.

The Nick of Time

Talent cannot be denied, so when Ariana got the part of Cat Valentine in Nickelodeon show *Victorious* when she was just 16, a star was born. The show's first-ever episode aired in March 2010 with Nickelodeon's second highest viewing figures for a live action series: 5.7 million, making Ari an overnight celebrity.

Never forget - Ariana and Jennette.

SMALL SCREEN QUEEN

Before she fully committed to music, Ariana had some unforgettable TV moments

Sam & Cat

If Joey and Phoebe from *Friends* had a daughter, chances are she'd be just like Cat Valentine – the ditziest kook in the cabbage patch. Her portrayal of an adorably crazy redhead was the real star of *Victorious* so naturally she got her own spin-off show with *iCarly*'s Sam Puckett (Jennette McCurdy). Cat was the purrrrfect showcase for Ariana's gift for comedy.

HAIRSPRAY LIVE

Ariana was such a fan of the *Hairspray* musical that when she heard they were doing a production for TV, she let it be known that she would do anything to appear in it and the producers must have thought all their Christmases came at once. In the made-for-TV film, Ari unleashes her dorky side as Tracy Turnblad's best friend Penny.

3 PURRRFECTLY VALID CAT VALENTINE QUESTIONS

"Did you hear what my giraffe just said? He's so inappropriate."

"Is it true that sweat and pee are, like, cousins?"

"Does my thumb look Spanish?"

Scream Queens

As a lover of scary movies, it made sense when Ari appeared in teen horror show *Scream Queens*. Ari played Sonya Herfmann aka Chanel #2, in six episodes. After being murdered she returns from hell uttering the genius line: "Yes there are water slides but they're lined with razorblades and you splash down into a pool of boiling pee. Also, zero

Macarons in human form. Wicked delicious

ANATOMY OF A POP PRINCESS

How does Ms Grande look (and smell) so good? This is how. Let's get ready with Ari

"I have just always worn my hair [in a ponytail] because it's super easy, so I suppose it kind of unintentionally became my signature look."

The original inspiration for Ariana's side pony came from the movie 13 Going On 30.

"My personal style is always evolving slightly, but slowly, but surely."

"I do mine [eyeliner] horribly every day. Trust me it's horrible. Some days my cat eye looks amazing and I'm like, I killed it. I like to do my liner, it's fun and it feels good. I learned from my mum who literally does her whole face of make-up in the car."

"I'm a fragrance girl, I love perfumes, I love body sprays and lotions."

"If you are as petite as I am, heels really help make an outfit."

"You know what I actually use on my body as well as my face? I feel like people would think it would make you break out, but it doesn't make you break out: coconut oil! Like, cooking oil. I put it everywhere—in my hair, on my body. It's the answer."

"I never really share the meanings behind my tattoos because tattoos are so personal. I have a bunch that I feel like people haven't seen yet because they're secretive and small. One of my favourites is the crescent moon on the side of my neck."

Ari feels her cosiest when she's wearing yoga leggings, slippers a crop top and a hoodie.

What's in Ariana's handbag?
Glasses, lip balm, hand sanitiser, and cayenne pepper – to spice up vegetables and hummus.

"Be yourself and don't listen to any trends. If you happen to like something that is trendy, cool—but just because it's 'in' at the time doesn't mean that you have to jump on the bandwagon. Being yourself is one of the coolest things that you can do."

THAT VOICE THOUGH

Think of a pop star with a better voice than Ariana Grande. It's OK, we'll wait ...

ARIANA GRANDE-BUTERA

Katy Perry has said that Ariana has the best female vocal in pop music and who's going to argue? When you start your career as an eight-year-old singing the national anthem before an ice hockey game (left), you can't just serve dimples, you have to have talent. Fast forward a couple of years and Ariana's selling out arenas and singing for president Barack Obama. So guess what? This girl has got serious pipes.

According to Ariana, growing up in Florida, which is warm, by the sea, and has humid air, was good for her voice.

DRIVE TIME

Joan Grande discovered her daughter's amazing talent one day when Ariana started singing in the car when she was about four or five. "My mum was like 'Do that again.' And she was like 'Oh my God, you can really sing!" When they got home Joan showed the whole family what little Ari could do and the rest is history.

Despite her 4-octave range, Ariana says it takes more work to go down to the lower register as her voice is naturally high.

When Ariana wants to protect her voice she sometimes speaks in a higher register to protect her vocal chords.

Bey B One More Time

One of the biggest vocal inspirations for Ariana was Beyoncé: "That's where I discovered my range," she revealed. "I grew up listening to Destiny's Child. I would try so hard to mimic all Beyoncé's little runs and ad-lib things. They are so precise. It's like math." ***Flawless.

Ariana's vocal coach Eric Vetro has also given lessons to Shawn Mendes, Camila Cabello and Katy Perry.

FANFARE!

Ariana loves three things beginning with the letter F: furry creatures, family and her FANS!!!

Arianator. *Noun.*
Definition: Someone who stans Ariana harder, harder, harder than any other pop star.

Wherefore art though, Ariana?

Signing autographs, taking selfies, collecting teddy bears.

MUM'S THE WORD

Ariana doesn't just appreciate her fans (they do pay her bills after all) she thinks of them as her children, "I feel a motherly attachment to them. I wish I could instil in them the things that my mom tries to instil in me."

Friends or fans?

There's a thin line between fan and friend for Ariana, so much so she considers some of her favourite fans, friends. She even has some of their phone numbers so she can call them up for a chat – and sometimes play them exclusive new music. Can you imagine? Don't scream.

When Ariana starts laughing the fans start snapping.

The Grabby Awards

Ari's fans love to get up close with their idol, sometimes a little bit too close. "It's love," she says, "sometimes they will grab you and I get scared very easily with something like that. But I love them for it and I love it."

GRANDE GIVES BACK

"If my fans want something, I'll always do my best to give it to them," Ariana confesses, and she did exactly that when she put out the song *Boyfriend Material* that didn't make the cut from the *Yours Truly* sessions. Arianators love classic Ari – so she mines the vault and gives them what they want. Ur welcome.

Beware the Hug monster - rarrr!!!

ARIANA IS AWWW-SOME

Even strong independent women enjoy big hugs from a giant chipmunk

A-DORA-BLE

DISNEY PRINCESS

Ariana was shocked to discover that the flamenco emoji was actually Dora The Explorer.

When you grow up in Florida, Mickey Mouse is basically your mayor.

PRIMATES ON PARADE

Monkeys are cute, lilac is one of Ariana's favourite colours, so when she met this guy on the Macy's Thanksgiving Day Parade of course there was love.

STOCKING FILLER

Q: What did Santa Claus ask for last Christmas?
A: Ariana Grande!
Wishes do come true.

YOU'RE ALVIN A LAUGH

Ariana was over the moon about the Jonas Brothers reunion, but the lack of trousers was a concern.

GOT HER NUMBER

Wanna know what makes Ariana great?
Let's figure it out.

16·9 MILLION

The streams *7 Rings* had in its first week – breaking the UK record

7

The number of dogs Ariana currently has: Toulouse, Coco, Cinnamon, Strauss, Lafayette Pignoli and Myron

36

Number of episodes of *Sam & Cat*

5

The number of UK number ones Ariana has had: *Bang Bang, Problem, Thank U, Next, 7 Rings* and *Break Up With Your Girlfriend I'm Bored*

$71 MILLION

Amount Grande's *Dangerous Woman* tour made

4

Octaves – the vocal range Ariana has. It's the reason she can hit those bird-trilling high notes

13

The name of the Broadway musical Ariana starred in before she got her break in *Victorious*. She played Charlotte the cheerleader

2

The number *One Last Time* reached in the chart, despite being Ariana's biggest-selling hit

$50 MILLION

The amount Ariana is reportedly worth

76

The number of countries where Ariana's second Album, *My Everything*, went to number one

10%

The amount of her hair that Ariana once joked was actually hers

$150 MILLION

Amount Ariana's three fragrances made in two years

2 stands for the buns on Ari's head and the number of times she was hit by an ice hockey puck as a kid.

6.30am

The time Ariana likes to wake up in the morning

93

The number of "Yuhs" on the *Thank U, Next* album – there are about 80 on *Sweetener*

ARI TALKS ...

There's so much going on inside Ariana's head, if only there was a way to discover what it was

... LOVE

"I'm such a romantic. I'm so traditional when it comes to that stuff. Love, for me, is laughter, respect, good conversation, genuine support, and more laughter."

... BEING A GEEK

"I'm a big nerd.
I love *Lord of the Rings*.
I love *Harry Potter*.
I love scary movies.
I love dinosaurs, science, aliens, ghosts."

... HER FEARS

"The littlest things freak me out. Like swallowing pills, people being sick. And I can't stand germs. I'm terrified of looking straight into the camera. I see people on the other side of the lens and the whole judgemental world of pop culture waiting with their pitchforks and torches."

... INSECURITY

"Insecurity has been the hardest thing I've had to overcome. I think everyone my age struggles with that because everyone strives for approval."

... EMBARRASSMENT

"I don't get easily embarrassed because I don't take myself seriously to begin with, so it takes a lot for me to be embarrassed. I'll be the first one to laugh at myself."

... BOSSING IT

"I didn't care about the business part for a very long time. Now I can confidently say that I run my show entirely from top to bottom. I realised how not okay I am with putting everything in someone else's hands. I have to think about everything, and it's a full-time job."

... BREAK-UPS

"Having your heart broken is awful but you have two choices: you can sulk or you can choose to remain positive. Stay positive that you'll fall in love again."

7 OF THE BEST
SINGLES

It's almost impossible to choose, but if we must ...

The Way

Ariana's first proper single after *Put Your Hearts Up* (which Ari would rather forget) was not a hit in the UK – madness – and sounds just as relevant today as it did six years ago. The breathy R&B jam, which looked back to the '90s before anyone else was doing it, is a shoulder-popping finger-clicking example of Ariana in her early Mariah-influenced phase – hello whistle tones.

Love Me Harder

Despite not being one of Ariana's biggest hits, this slow building eruption of propulsive electro pop is easily one of her best, with Ariana's sweet and warm vocals bathing our ears in echoey joy. This one comes courtesy not only of The Weeknd, who shares vocal duties with Ari, but super writer/producers Max Martin and Savan Kotecha – her literal 'write hand man.'

Problem

If this song was a Friends episode it would be called *The One With The Horns.* This brassy explosion of pop was Ariana's first UK number one and features Australian rapper Iggy Azalea and Ari at her shrieking best. A rat-a-tat stutter of sixties funk crammed with tricks, ticks and sirens is an assault on the senses and it's not a problem at all.

Into You

Like many of Ariana's songs, this Martin/Kotecha epic is jam-packed with drama. From a super-slow building start, it cranks the suspense like a roller coaster, before peaking into a crunchy chorus of dirty bass and Ariana's most angelic soprano. This is the sound of midnight infatuation through smoke machines and lasers at the world's best nightclub – just try standing still when you hear it.

Dance to This

The mellowest banger ever is actually a Troye Sivan song featuring Ariana, and it's too damn good. Why wasn't this a massive whopping great hit? It has over 100 million views on YouTube but only got to 64 in the chart – blame radio. Ariana has sung a bunch of duets but this sultry, skittery, sad disco moment has more #FEELS than any of them.

Dangerous Woman

A moody mid-tempo track that borders on an all out chugging rock sing-a-long and you can totally imagine Ariana swinging her pony and strutting on stage in a sweaty bar. The grown-up sound was a departure for Ariana and it still sounds unique in her catalogue. Fun fact: Charlie Puth beatboxes at the beginning of the track.

7 Rings

The song Ariana describes as a friendship anthem borrows its tune from *The Sound of Music*'s *Favourite Things* and consequently Ari has to give a whopping 90% of all royalties to the estate of Rogers and Hammerstein. Was it worth it? Of course. You betcha. Once this deceptively-simple, record-breaking ode to retail therapy gets stuck in your head it's there for days – seventh heaven.

BORN TO
PERFORM

She may be tiny to the point of being invisible,
but Ariana belongs on a stage, end of!

When you've got a voice like Ariana, going to see her live is all about that incredible vocal, but that's not *all* you get. Ari puts on a spectacular show packed with cool costume changes, slinky dance routines, elaborate set pieces and general audio-visual hoopla – all while sounding flawless. Ariana has

had four headlining concert tours, but her first major tour was as the opening act for Justin Bieber in 2013. Since then, as she's got bigger and better, so have her shows. She sang a breezy 11 songs on her first tour, *The Listening Sessions*, but on her *Sweetener World Tour*, the set-list swelled to a massive 29 songs – which is a pretty sweet deal.

The *Dangerous Woman Tour* opened with a super slick and stylish voguing routine.

You can see how much effort Ariana puts into her shows by how much her ponytail moves. Basically it's a superstar in its own right.

Ariana's ears prick up at the Hollywood Bowl.

Scott and Brian Nicholson – or 'the twins' as Ariana calls them – have been back-up dancers for Ari since forever. They also appeared in the videos such as *Baby I, Break Free* and *Thank You, Next*.

✴ Setlist for Ariana's ✴ 2019 SWEETENER TOUR

* Raindrops (An Angel Cried)
* God Is a Woman
* Bad Idea
* Break Up With Your Girlfriend, I'm Bored
* R.E.M.
* Be Alright 👁
* Sweetener
  * Successful
  * Side to Side
  * Bloodline
* 7 Rings
* Love Me Harder
* Breathin
* Needy
* Fake Smile

* Make Up
* Right There
* You'll Never Know
* Break Your Heart Right Back
* NASA
* Goodnight n Go
* In My Head
* Everytime
* One Last Time
* The Light Is Coming
* Into You
* Dangerous Woman
* Break Free
* No Tears Left to Cry !!!
* Thank U, Next

Ari's greatest fashion hit? Her Vera Wang, Met Gala, Sistine Chapel eleganza. Divine.

FASHION ICON

ON A SCALE OF 1-10, SHE'S 100

Ariana is ALL about the music, but damn she looks good doing it

Ariana Grande is flawless – look at her, she's virtually edible – but it took a while to get there. Like all young girls, she experimented with fashion before finding a style that suited her. It's been a long journey from goofy teen actor to the biggest pop star on the planet but she always looked cute doing it.

From the early years where Ariana had red hair and a never-ending wardrobe of perky '50s florals, to her love of Audrey Hepburn and Marie Antoinette, through to today's tomboy sweats and oversized off-the-shoulder puffas, she's always known how to work her diminutive proportions.

Her style is unapologetic, she doesn't care what anyone thinks. If she wants to dress like a Disney princess she will, if she fancies a casual day in boys' clothes, then guess what ...? In fact, one of her biggest style inspirations is a boy, well, a man: Pharrell Williams. "I literally buy everything I see him wearing," she said in a recent interview, "He's like Regina George, and I'm Cady Heron (from the film *Mean Girls*). I don't believe clothing has any sort of gender specifics — I want to shop in the boys' section."

ARI SAYS

"I'm always drawn to things that are slightly retro and I love an animal ear, clearly."

FASHION FOCUS

It took a hot minute, but now everything Ariana wears is a 'moment'

JEAN DREAMY
When it comes to style, Ariana is a complex mix of hyper-feminine and gender neutral, loving slouchy athleisure as much as cute dresses. The baggy pants and deconstructed jean jacket showcase her approachable side.

YOLKING AROUND
Ariana lets her hair down and cleverly coordinates her tangerine bodycon dress to the Nickelodeon colour palette, but the Chanel Rugrats cartoon handbag steals the show.

SHOWER PUFF GIRL
As she gets older Ariana has become more experimental making some bolder style choices like the lavender 'loofah' dress she wore to Billboard's Women in Music event in 2018.

C'MON BARBIE ...

Old school Ari was a sucker for skater skirts and girly colours. This punchy pink number says pop star on the go and makes her legs look loooong even though she's petite.

GRANDE DESIGNS

All celebs love a designer label and Ariana is no exception. Sure she'll rock Reebok, but she'll also throw on a Moschino dress, pair it with some signature over-the-knee boots, and – BOOM – she's red carpet ready.

MERMAZING

It's all or nothing for Ariana, who either goes for a floor length gown or thigh-skimming mini. This gorgeous red Romona Keveza princess fantasy was teamed with bright white jewels and a dark smoky eye for extra drama.

7 ALBUMS
RANKED

Putting your loves in order is a cruel business

Thank U, Next

The most Ariana album yet – a confident expression and consolidation of everything that came before, encompassing the playful surprises of *Sweetener* and the melodic power of *My Everything*. It sounds utterly beautiful, dramatic, atmospheric, funky, fun and catchy with some powerful proclamations, flipping between R&B, reggae, hip-hop, trap, and pristine pop. Ariana wrote and recorded it in a matter of weeks!!!

My Everything

Ariana's first absolutely-essential album. A pop masterpiece, *My Everything* is Ari at the peak of pop perfection. It gave her number one hits around the world and elevated her position of global icon alongside Taylor Swift, Rihanna and Katy Perry. She released five singles off the record, each one as good as the last: *Problem, Break Free, Bang, Bang, Love Me Harder* and *One Last Time*.

Dangerous Woman

Dangerous Woman was Ariana's first album to go to number one in the UK, spawning mega hits *Side to Side, Into You* and of course *Dangerous Woman*. This record saw Ariana coming out of her shell, showcasing her true authentic self with anthems of empowerment like mellow confessional *I Don't Care*, and bangers like *Greedy* and *Sometimes*.

Sweetener

The upside-down artwork gives you a clue to the fact that Ari is about to turn everything you expect on its head. Perhaps after the tragic Manchester attacks Ariana didn't feel like making a full-tilt pop record, so what we get is washes of experimentation, vibing and getting down to the groove rather than serving straight up karaoke classics. Ari delivers some real shocks amid the hits.

Yours Truly

Ariana launched her career with a throwback retro 90s sound, working with producer Babyface, the veteran writer/producer of hits for artists like Whitney Huston, Toni Braxton and TLC. The songs are strong with some all-time classics. *Honeymoon Avenue* is a forever keeper, but *Yours Truly* is pretty much the sound of Ariana finding her feet artistically.

Christmas & Chill + Christmas Kisses

If you combine these two EPs you get the perfect ten-track Christmas album. *Christmas & Chill* is great – in the tradition of Destiny's Child's classic festive album, it's a smooth 90s inspired R&B winter warmer. The Aaliyah-inspired *Wit It This Christmas* is a bop! The best of *Christmas Kisses* is a beautiful ballad *Snow in California* where Ariana channels Britney.

The Remix

This Japan-only remix album offered some alternative dance mixes of the singles from Ariana's first two albums. If you're having a party and want to switch things up, this is a brilliant way to do it. Try the super speedy *Baby I Cosmic Dawn* radio edit, *Right There 7th Heaven Radio* edit or the rave-tastic Gazzo remix of *One Last Time*, that takes you straight to a midnight beach party.

ARI SAYS

"If I'm going to be a role model, the last thing I should be is perfect because that's not realistic. As long as I'm honest and genuine and I share with my fans my truest self, that's the best that I can do because that's allowing them to do the same thing."

KEEPING IT REAL

Ariana's no stuck up star – she's down to earth, honest, and as insecure as the rest of us

She may appear to live the dream glamorous celeb lifestyle, drinking champagne at Tiffany's and buying whatever she wants, but Ariana is more normal than you might think. She doesn't go to loads of swanky parties, preferring to chill at home in comfy clothes with her puppies, doing face packs, bingeing Netflix and reliving the trials of Harry Potter. She has the same insecurities as most girls and doesn't think she's all that. She's basically you.

If Ariana wants to be cosy in a onesie, no one is going to stop her.

ANGST, YOU? NEXT.

Although she seems to have the perfect life, Ariana admits to having anxiety, even going so far as to joke: "My anxiety has anxiety." Just because she can get on a stage in front of thousands of people, doesn't mean that some days aren't a struggle for her.

Ari's endorsements speak to the fans. First she promoted Lipsy, the cute fashion retailer, then Reebok, the sportswear brand beloved of UK high street, and in March 2019 she became a Starbucks ambassador, launching her very own 'cloud macchiato' – dreamy.

Snap unhappy

If it looks like Ariana is a natural, posing and pouting for the cameras at fancy events, she might not be having the best time: "I just want to make music and entertain people, I am not very comfortable walking red carpets and having my photo taken," Ari once said.

THANK U, EX

Of course the boys that work with Ariana fall for her – and she loves them right back!

GRAHAM PHILLIPS

Ariana met *Riverdale* actor Graham when they both starred in the musical 13 when she was 15. They dated from 2008 to 2011,

but they met up for a nice Italian dinner as recently as March 2019.

JAI BROOKS

When we first fell in love with Ari, she was an item with Jai Brooks, one of the members of YouTube prankster Aussies, Janoskians. She loves goofy guys and that was Jai to a tee.

NATHAN SYKES

Remember The Wanted, the boyband that tried and failed to match One Direction's enormous success? Like Ariana, they were repped by Scooter Braun, so of course Ari ended up falling for cutest member Nathan.

THANK U, NEXT

BIG SEAN

Like Nathan, Big Sean worked on a song with Ariana for her debut album, and there must have been chemistry because they started dating in 2014, hitting the red carpet together at the 2015 Grammys!

RICKY ALVAREZ

Pop stars love to date their dancers, and Ari is no exception. She got snogsy with Ricky for about a year before they split in 2016. He gets an epic name check in *Thank U, Next* "Wrote some songs about Ricky, now I listen and laugh." Cute.

THANK U, NEXT

MAC MILLER

Mac was the third artist to collab on Ari's debut and then date her. They got together in 2016 and dated for about two years. When he passed away in September 2018, Ariana was completely devastated.

PETE DAVIDSON

Ariana and *SNL* funny guy Pete fell hard for each other, getting engaged just weeks after they hooked up, but perhaps it wasn't to be, because Ariana called the whole thing off. This love business is hard.

THANK U, NEXT

MY FAMILY, MY EVERYTHING

Families can be tricky, but not for Ariana because she totally adores hers!

The Family Grande, all dressed up in 2011.

Can I be Frank?

Out of everyone in her family, Ari's grandpa Frank, who passed away in 2014, holds a special place in her heart. "He was the person I was closest to in my life. He was everything I wanted to be: as a businessman, as a gentleman, as a human being, as a friend. He was just perfect to me."

Mum's the word

Ariana's mum is not just incredibly caring and cool, she's a boss when it comes to fashion. "My mom is fly, she's the baddest. My whole life, she's always worn custom-made, black, tailored outfits. Black only – I've never seen her wear another colour."

Taking Control

It wasn't all easy going for Ariana growing up: "My parents were very protective and controlling for a lot of my life but at the same time I know that they were doing it for my own good."

Big Brother

He may be nearly ten years older than Ariana, but Frankie Grande and his sister are devoted to each other. They regularly performed together growing up – *Suddenly Seymour* is a fave duet – they hang out together, go to events, go shopping and Ariana says that she learned loads from Frankie, who used to sneak her into places when she was growing up. "I had an older brother who always managed to get me into things that I wanted to go to but that made me feel safe and secure as he was always with me."

Ariana loves to cook with her family, making favourites like zucchini pasta – that's courgette to you and me.

Frankie lends his support while Ari promotes her perfume, also called Ari.

DADDY ISSUES

Despite the joy her family brings her, it's not all plain sailing for Ari, who has bravely spoken about falling out of touch with her dad. "So much of me comes from my father, and for so long, I didn't like that about myself. I had to accept that it's okay not to get along with somebody and still love them."

41

ARIANA IS YOUR LIFE COACH

Stop being so *needy* and *focus* on the *problem* because *the light is coming!*

★ Ignore gossip

"I used to freak out about everything all the time. I used to be like, 'Oh my God, somebody said this!' Everything used to be such a big deal! But now, I feel I can handle everything that comes my way with a calm energy."

★ Ask for help

"In all honesty, therapy has saved my life so many times. If you're afraid to ask for help, don't be. You don't have to be in constant pain and you can process trauma. I've got a lot of work to do, but it's a start to even be aware that it's possible."

★ Be kind to yourself

"It's been part of my personal growth to be a little nicer to myself. Everyone needs to be a little nicer to themselves. We're all hard on ourselves. I've learnt so much about all that. It's so hard for women not to be critical about themselves when there's such a high bar set for what is acceptable."

★ Step away from your phone

"I think we all spend a bit too much time on our social devices when we could be spending time with the people in front of us. It can be unhealthy. We need to maintain a healthy brain space outside of that internet world."

★ Acknowledge what you have

"You should feel grateful and happy that you're healthy, you're alive, and that you are loved. Whatever weight you are, whatever situation you're in, whether you have a breakout, whatever it is – you are loved."

★ Follow your own path

"I don't want to do what people tell me to do, I don't want to conform to the pop star agenda. I want to do it on my own terms from now on. If I want to tour two albums at once, I'm going to tour two albums at once. If I want to drop a third album while I'm on tour, I'll do that too."

7 OF THE BEST
MUSIC VIDEOS

Counting down the best of Ari's mini movies

1

Thank U, Next
This broke the YouTube record for most views in 24 hours with 55.4 million views and it's easy to see why. The breezy breakup song brilliantly parodies teen movies like *Mean Girls, Bring It On* and *Legally Blonde* with a star-studded cast including Troye Sivan, Colleen Ballinger and Jennifer Coolidge.

2

God is a Woman
The most elaborate, bonkers and amazing Ariana video there is. First she's in a pool of primordial goop, then she's a bear, a candle, she's doing yoga on the earth, she's a tightrope walker, a renaissance fresco – and then there's the screaming gophers. Genius certainly comes in many forms.

3

No Tears Left to Cry
The concept of this freaky dystopian vision is pretty deep: that the world is a topsy-turvy place with everything flipped upside down and sideways. Just like life in the 21st century, it can be hard to make sense of things. Also, if God is a woman, she doesn't walk on water, she crawls down walls.

4

Break Free

The *Break Free* video is a campy spoof of ropey sci-fi movies like *Barbarella* and *Flash Gordon*, featuring giant robots, lizard monsters and a nifty rocket-launching brassiere. A visual effect-laden romp; so good you'll soil yourself from intergalactic excitement (her words not ours).

5

Side to Side

This video is truly iconic, and not just because of Ari's hat. It's pretty much impossible to hear this song without imagining yourself at a neon-lit spin class cycling your way to a fitter, better you. It's definitely one of Ariana's saucier videos which is maybe why it has over a billion and a half views. Phew.

6

Right There

Ariana lives out her Hollywood fantasies in a loose reworking of Shakespeare's *Romeo and Juliet* – guess which part Ari plays? The vibe is 18th century France meets 1980s Miami pool party and it's a full-on production. Slick, sweet and romantic, basically the Ferrero Rocher of M/Vs.

7

Focus

The star of this video is Ariana's grey-blonde wig, a look she obviously loves and keeps coming back to. Pretty much a straight-forward performance video with no gimmicks (apart from the do), just singing, dancing, looking stunning – putting all the FOCUS on Ariana. It's quite clever really.

YOU FUNNY, ARI

Cat Valentine was a genius next-level LOLatron,
but so is IRL Ariana – like all the time

MAKES NO SCENTS

Ariana really, really, REALLY loves her own perfume.

TROPHY OR NOT TROPHY?

No matter how hard she wishes, Ariana cannot turn this award into an Oscar.

BOAT OF NO CONFIDENCE

Boats aren't for everyone. There's the seasickness, the slowness, the confusion about starboard and port – it's a lot.

GHOSTIN' GRANDE

She's had a few boyfriends, but did you know that Ariana once dated the invisible man?

WIGGIN' OUT

When Ari appeared as She-Ra on SNL with Chris Pratt as He-Man, she smashed it. No really, she totally destroyed the place.

ANGEL OR DEVIL?

When you're teeny tiny and a giant model nearly knocks you over with her massive great wings and you grit your teeth and duck and cover. That.

GET READY WITH ME...

Wanna look as good as Ms Grande?

Here's how she does it

When it comes to lips, Ari loves Mac Viva Glam or Chapstick.

Side to side eye

Ariana admits that her look is all about the eyes. Specifically a precision winged eyeliner cat eye: "It took forever but I think I'm there. I mastered it by practice and prayer." Ari says the look was inspired by her rock chick mum and Scary Spice.

A PONY'S TALE

Nothing comes between Ariana Grande and her ponytail: she's been swishing it since she was at school and says it still brings her joy. "Every time I put my hair up, it's like a surprise and I'm like, 'I love this look! Ooh, girl!' It's like true love."

ARI SAYS

"I use my hair as a mask, as a shield. I hide behind it and it's what keeps me, me."

ARIANA'S BEAUTY TIPS

- **Drink lots of water**
- **Wash your face with cold water**
- **Exfoliate**
- **Always take your make-up off before bed**
- **Get plenty of sleep**

Let it shine

Ariana's famous ponytail is treated to sweet silky loving courtesy of a whole lot of oil. Moroccan oil, coconut oil even lavender essential oil, she went so far as to gush: "I love putting lavender on my head." A sweetener indeed.

ARI'S BFFs
(BEST FAMOUS FRIENDS)

If you were to take a sneaky scroll through Ariana's phone, who might you find next to 'mom'?

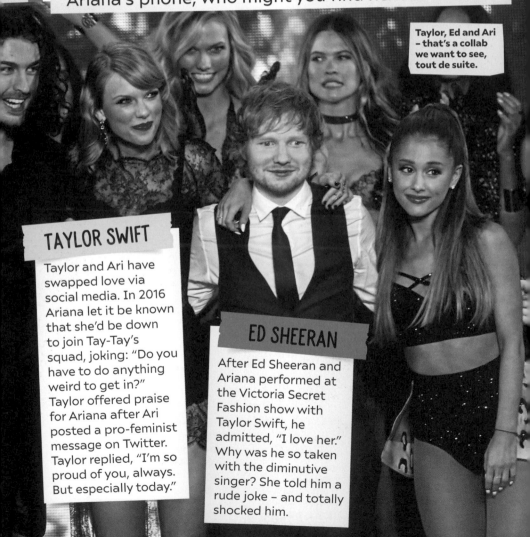

Taylor, Ed and Ari – that's a collab we want to see, tout de suite.

TAYLOR SWIFT

Taylor and Ari have swapped love via social media. In 2016 Ariana let it be known that she'd be down to join Tay-Tay's squad, joking: "Do you have to do anything weird to get in?" Taylor offered praise for Ariana after Ari posted a pro-feminist message on Twitter. Taylor replied, "I'm so proud of you, always. But especially today."

ED SHEERAN

After Ed Sheeran and Ariana performed at the Victoria Secret Fashion show with Taylor Swift, he admitted, "I love her." Why was he so taken with the diminutive singer? She told him a rude joke – and totally shocked him.

Whenever Nicki and Ari work together, things go off with a bang, bang!

NICKI MINAJ

Nicki has worked with Ariana a number of times and Ari says she adores her as an artist and as a person, "Literally, the things I would do for her. She's very real. I could tell her about anything and she'd be ready to listen." While Nicki says of Ari, "You've been there for me behind the scenes. Love you for life." Awww, you two.

HARRY POTTER CAST

Ariana's patronus is J.K. Rowling – she adores Harry Potter and has hung out with cast members such as Daniel Radcliffe, Rupert Grint, Tom Felton and Matthew Lewis.

Ari met Rupert Grint at the *Deathly Hallows Part 2* premiere.

Katy Perry

Katy has been supportive of Ariana from the start with Ari calling her "welcoming and wonderful", so they're good enough mates to take the mickey out of each other on social media. After one post on Instagram, Katy teased, "Can you just put on your jacket once please, just once." How did Ari react? With one word, "No." Pop star lols.

Selena Gomez

Selena may be Disney and Ari might be Nickelodeon but there's no beef between the ex-teen TV stars. When Ariana told reporters on the red carpet that she'd just seen Selena Gomez, she said: "She looks like a princess. I literally almost cried when I saw her, I haven't talked to her in a long time, but I gave her a huge hug and I'm so happy that she's here."

Harry Styles

A couple of years ago Harry Styles wrote a song for Ariana Grande and in 2019 he followed her on Instagram, sending the internet into gossipy meltdown. She's also spent time at the London home of former One Direction star Niall Horan.

Justin Bieber

Because Justin Bieber and Ariana share a manager, Scooter Braun, inevitably they are on friendly terms. They've performed together, hung out in the studio and regularly support each other on social media.

ONE, TWO, THREE, SAY 'BRIE!'

INSTAGRANDE

Ariana owns, kills, and slays social media, and we are mere followers

Follow your leader

Wanna see what Ari sees? Here are some of the Instagram accounts she follows: Britney Spears, Jennette McCurdy, Patrick Starrr, Dove Cameron, Dua Lipa, all of Little Mix, Hailey Bieber, Colleen Ballinger, Zendaya, Lush Cosmetics, Emma Watson, Michelle Obama, Starbucks, Shangela from *RuPaul's Drag Race*, NASA, Steve The Dog, and her mum Joan Grande.

Ari's selfie tip: Be honest

Don't make up elaborate or ridiculous captions for your pics, just lay out the truth.

"We all post a selfie for the same reason – because we feel better about ourselves than usual. So just be like, 'Hey, I feel good about myself today, so here's a picture!'" Preach.

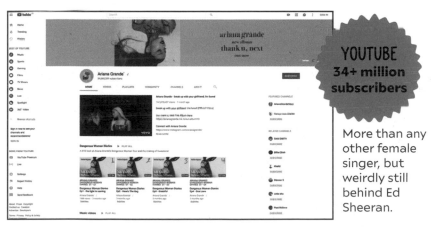

INSTAGRAM
148+ million followers

TWITTER
61+ million followers

YOUTUBE
34+ million subscribers

She is the most followed woman on Insta – BOOM. She overtook Selena Gomez in early 2019.

Ariana is a fantastic communicator, posting personal thoughts and pics all the time – over 44,000 times to be exact.

More than any other female singer, but weirdly still behind Ed Sheeran.

In case you haven't sussed it yet, Ariana loves black and white pictures, so fab up your Insta feed by giving Inkwell, Moon and Willow a go, too.

Throwback? More like throw up

Everyone cringes at old posts, even Ariana: "Oh my god! You know when you scroll a little too far back on your Facebook and you're like, 'Oh my god, oh my god – I didn't want to see that! Why am I going through this? I didn't mean to scroll that far!"

SURVIVOR

Despite everything, Ariana found the strength to go on and not let sadness and tragedy define her

After the Manchester attack of 2017, Ariana didn't cancel her tour, she took time off to grieve and try to come to terms with the tragic event, and then she went straight back to Manchester to perform a benefit concert for 55,000 people. The three-hour-plus event saw performances from Justin Bieber, Little Mix, Coldplay, Liam Gallagher, Pharrell Williams, Niall Horan and many more.

THE ONE LOVE CONCERT WAS STREAMED LIVE IN MORE THAN 50 COUNTRIES AND RAISED £18 MILLION FOR THE FAMILIES OF VICTIMS AND INJURED SURVIVORS

Justin Bieber came onstage alone and sang *Love Yourself* accompanied only with his acoustic guitar.

Song for Frank

When Ariana sang *Over the Rainbow*, it was incredibly moving, but the song was extra poignant for Ariana: the Judy Garland classic from *The Wizard of Oz* was a favourite of her Grandpa who had passed away three years before. He had always said that Ariana should close her concerts with the song, but she never did until that day.

Little Mix performed their uplifting debut single *Wings*.

AFTER THE MANCHESTER ATTACK ARIANA KEPT IN CONTACT WITH MANY FAMILIES OF THE VICTIMS

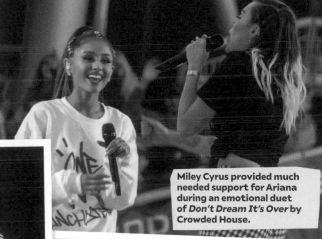

Miley Cyrus provided much needed support for Ariana during an emotional duet of *Don't Dream It's Over* by Crowded House.

The crowd joined Katy Perry in a stripped back rendition of hit song, *Part of Me*.

Self Care

Months after Manchester, her close friend and ex-boyfriend Mac Miller died, absolutely crushing Ariana. "I can't even say 'Good morning' to anyone without crying," she half joked. If there is a positive to all the pain, Ariana says that her priorities have changed. She lives life fearlessly and she's not sweating the small stuff. "I guess there's not much I'm afraid of anymore," she said, "I just want to be happy and healthy."

MTV

VID

MUS

AWA

MTV

IDEO

USIC

ARDS

Ariana picks up a 'moon man' trophy for *No Tears Left to Cry* – although she may have shed a few that night in New York.

YOU'RE A WINNER, BABY

You like her, you love her, gee thanks, she's flattered

★ American Music Awards

2013 New artist of the year
2015 Pop/rock female artist
2016 Artist of the year

★ Billboard Women in Music Awards

2018 Woman of the year

★ BRIT Awards

2019 Best female solo artist

★ Grammy Awards

2019 Best pop vocal album: *Sweetener*

★ MTV Europe Awards

2013 Best song: *Problem*
2014 Best female artist
2016 Best US act

★ MTV Video Music Awards

2014 Best pop video: *Problem*
2018 Best pop: *No Tears Left to Cry*

★ Nickelodeon Kids' Choice Awards

2014 Favourite TV actress: *Sam & Cat*
2015 Song of the year: *Bang, Bang*
2016 Female artists
2019 Favourite song: *Thank U, Next*
2019 Favourite female artist

★ People's Choice Awards

2014 Favourite breakout artist

★ Radio 1's Teen Awards

2017 Best international solo artist

★ Teen Choice Awards

2014 Choice female artist (below)
2014 Choice female single: *Problem*
2015 Choice song female artist: *One Last Time*
2015 Choice instagrammer
2016 Choice song female artist: *Dangerous Woman*
2016 Choice selfie taker
2017 Choice female artist
2017 Choice summer tour: *Dangerous Woman Tour*
2017 Choice snapchatter
2017 Choice change maker
2018 Choice snapchatter

★ YouTube Music Awards

2015 50 artists to watch

Forget seven rings, where on earth does Ari keep her 11 surfboards?

ARIANA THE
ACTIVIST

She's got a big voice, and guess what?
She's not afraid to use it!

Some celebrities avoid speaking about serious issues, for fear of losing fans, money or sounding dumb. Not Ariana Grande, she's vocal about all her beliefs and stands up for those with less power, to make noise where it's most needed. She has faced criticism but that won't silence her or stop her going on marches and demonstrating. "There's a lot of noise when you say anything about anything. Not everyone is going to agree with you, but that doesn't mean I'm just going to shut up and sing my songs."

Feminism
She may look adorable cartoon, but Ariana Grande is a grown woman, who refuses to be patronised by men who seek to diminish or belittle her. When asked to choose between make-up and her phone, she let it be known that lazy casual sexist thinking was not OK: "Boys learn ... You need a little brushing up on equality here."

LGBT+ ally
Ariana grew up singing in gay bars, her brother Frankie is gay, and she says that most of her friends are gay so of course she supports and stands up for the LGBT+ community. She's so supportive that fans sometimes come out to her at meet and greets.

Ariana uses her power and position to help others

Gun control

After the tragic shooting at Stoneman Douglas High School in Florida, Ariana not only performed at the March For Our Lives rally against gun violence, she met with survivors to share her experiences about the healing process after the Manchester bombing.

Black Lives Matter

In 2016 Ariana released a single *Better Days* with Victoria Monet that addressed a string of fatal shootings in Dallas Texas.

Animal rights

She adopts stray dogs, has stopped eating meat and using animal products and condemns the capture and use of sea mammals in theme parks, "No one wants to be in the bathtub for 60 years," she once said.

Gender identity

Like many of her generation, Ariana has said that she doesn't agree with stereotyping people based on their gender, "Boxing people in, labelling, it's all just really unnecessary. Women are so many things. Men are so many things. People are so many things."

THE TEN O'SHOCK

When you're a celeb, gossip lurks round every corner and Ariana has had her fair share of controversies!

SAM & CAT FIGHT

There were reports of a **brief beef between Jennette McCurdy** and Ariana, with Jennette supposedly refusing to go to the Kids' Choice Awards the year Ariana won Fave TV actress. Jennette denied it saying they, "butted heads ... but in a very sisterly way."
SHOCK RATING:

GRAMMY WHAMMY

When Ariana won her first Grammy Award in Feb 2019 but didn't go to the show, she was **accused of not being able to organise her performance** in time, which Ari denied, stating that she'd been creatively stifled.
SHOCK RATING:

OVER THE RAINBOW

Having a special relationship with the city, Ariana agreed to play Manchester Pride in 2019 but **faced a backlash** for not actually being LGBT and for driving up the price of tickets.
SHOCK RATING:

Jennette and Ariana fight it out.

BBQ TATTOO

When Ariana **had a tattoo in Japanese characters** to commemorate her new single, but instead of it reading '7 rings' it actually meant 'small charcoal grill' – ooh burn.
SHOCK RATING:

NEWS

WHAT A BOOB!

Ariana performed at the funeral of Aretha Franklin, and was **hugged so tightly by a pastor** that he was accused of touching her boob. He also compared her name to an item on a fast food menu.
SHOCK RATING:
⚡⚡⚡⚡⚡

ARIANA BAMBINA

It was widely reported that Ariana demanded to be **carried around like a baby**, but Ari confirmed that in actual fact she'd been dancing so hard that her feet were bleeding and a mate gave her a helping hoist.
SHOCK RATING:
⚡⚡⚡⚡⚡

'Oh my god, what are they saying now?'

SNAPPED?

Ariana is **accused of being a diva** who demands to have her photo taken from one angle, and for walking out of a photo shoot in Australia.
SHOCK RATING:
⚡⚡⚡⚡⚡

DOUGHNUTTER

Ariana puts the tip of her **tongue on a doughnut** in a shop and was blacklisted from performing at the White House as a result.
SHOCK RATING:
⚡⚡⚡⚡⚡

> **"** I live fast
> and full-out,
> and I make mistakes,
> and I learn from them
> and I'm grateful
> no matter what
> happens **"**

Ariana Grande

CREDITS

ALL PICTURES: Alamy